P9-ANZ-962

PRAYERS FOR WOMEN

I'M STILL LEARNING, LORD

BETTY STEELE EVERETT

Illustrated by
MARTHA BENTLEY

Judson Press® Valley Forge

I'M STILL LEARNING, LORD

Library of Congress Cataloging-in-Publication Data

Everett, Betty Steele, 1929–
  I'm still learning, Lord.

  1. Prayer. I. Title.
BV245.E78   1986   242   86-20995
ISBN 0-8170-1112-9

The name JUDSON PRESS is registered as a trademark in the U.S. Patent Office. Printed in the U.S.A.

Foreword

I have just reread Betty Steele Everett's book, *I'm Still Learning, Lord,* and have alternatively chuckled and cried throughout. Either she has experienced many of these modern traumas herself or she's an excellent listener for she has captured the emotions underlying each one.

Having just passed "The Big Five-O" myself, her prayer on that subject was timely:

> I am past the "rushing" years of youth;
> I know who I am now, Lord—
> A child of God.
> And I know what I can do well.
> And what I should leave to others.

What valuable knowledge that is!

Many women can testify that this new self-knowledge has led them onto strange new paths. In the title poem, "I'm Still Learning, Lord," the author says

> I wondered how it would feel to be older than most students' mothers.
> I wondered how it would feel to be older than the professor!

It does indeed feel strange as many of us can testify.

Who among us with children who have left home cannot resonate with these lines:

> We left our "baby" on a doorstep today, Lord.
> Oh, not as a foundling, but as a college freshman.
> I felt as though I was abandoning her, though . . .
> Or that she was abandoning me.

Whether or not we have children, we all have (or had) parents. These poignant lines strike a cord for anyone who has watched the mental and/or physical deterioration of a parent:

> She's my mother, Lord. She's seventy-eight years old,
> And today I took her to a nursing home.
> I thought of so many things, Lord.
> I remembered the dresses she sewed for me when I was young.
> Now it takes her an hour to dress herself,
> And then some of the buttons are in the wrong holes.
> She cared for me when I was young and could not care for myself.
> Now I feel that I'm letting her down because I can't take care of her when she is the child.
> What should I do, Lord?
> What would You do?

The Scripture that helped Ms. Everett resolve her conflict (John 19:26–27) is one that I have used many times in my own work with families of the aged.

Sometimes grief moves in and takes seemingly permanent possession of our lives. There's the grief of losing a sibling:

> I always took care of her, Lord,
> Protected her from the bigger kids,
> And led her past the neighborhood dogs.
> Now I can't break the path for her to follow, Lord.
> She is going to do something first—
> The biggest thing of all.
> She is going to die before I do.

There's the special ache we suffer when a grown son or daughter is in trouble, laid off or divorced.

The author includes the grief of moving to a new home in a new state:

> I can't help thinking about the old.
> I don't want to have to find a new church, Lord;

Our present church is like a family to us.
I don't want to have to find new stores for shopping,
A new beauty parlor,
A new doctor and dentist,
New friends.

Ms. Everett touches on relationships between married and single women, on competition between grandparents and on being a stepgrandparent, on being a mother-in-law, and on being the spouse of a retiree. In "What's to Become of Us, Lord?" she echos some of the fears of all of us concerning the future:

You promised Noah that you would never destroy the world again with water, Lord;
You said nothing about an atomic war that we humans start.
What will happen to my grandchildren then, Lord? . . .
What about the earth itself, Lord?
Will there be pure water for them to drink?
Will there be fuels to keep them warm?
Will there be enough food to maintain life?
Will there be trees, flowers and grass for them to enjoy?

Ms. Everett's prayers are modern psalms for women. The anguish and grief, the joy and faith they express serve as touchstones for our own lives. Enjoy!

Dr. Carol S. Pierskalla
Director, Aging Today and Tomorrow
National Ministries
American Baptist Churches in the U.S.A.

Contents

Introduction

I have now passed the halfway mark in my life. In talking to friends my age, and women slightly older and younger, I have found that we have many of the same feelings about life as we mature.

God has brought us to the halfway place in our lives by many different routes. Some have been easy roads; others harder. All of us have lived through problems and pains, pleasures and privileges.

Now we are finding that the second half of our lives has more similarities than the first half did. We face many of the same situations. We enjoy many of the same things, things we did not have thirty years ago and would have been too busy and too immature to enjoy if we had had them.

In this short book of prayer devotions I have tried to deal with both problems and pleasures. I have tried to include many different ones, as suggested by my life and the lives of my friends.

One of the greatest pleasures and privileges of the second half of life is that of knowing the Lord in a deeper, more committed, more personal way. Now we have the time to read His Word in depth, to come closer to Paul's ideal of praying without ceasing, to work more often in His church on earth, and to give more money to His work for others.

This closeness to God takes away the fears of possible pains and problems. It heightens the enjoyment of our second half of life.

I pray these prayer devotions will help you in your walk with God and help you to enjoy the second half of life even more than you enjoyed the first half.

Experience Does Count, Lord

I have never been an important person, Lord,
Except to my family and close friends—and You.
But today I felt important.
Today I found that experience does count
Because I am old enough to know things the young haven't
    learned yet.
And I'm old enough to be trusted.
I was in the mall, standing by the center fountain.
A young woman, barely more than a child herself,
Came along, pushing a stroller.
The little boy in it was crying
And fussing as though he was tired and lonely.
The young mother looked so distraught, Lord,
As she tried to comfort him.
Then she saw I was watching her.
At first her face got red,
But when I smiled at her, she smiled back.
"He's tired," she told me.
"We've been here too long.
But I have one more thing to buy—
A present for my husband."
She was holding the baby now,
Patting him on the back and cooing softly.
"I guess I'll just have to carry him," she said.
She reached for the handle of the empty stroller,
And I could see she would have trouble doing everything.
She would not be able to look for her husband's gift easily,
And a wife should have time to choose such a gift.
"Let me hold him," I said suddenly.

I wasn't planning to say it, Lord;
It just came out.
Her face brightened. "Would you? Would you really?"
"I'll come with you," I told her.
"You push the stroller, and I'll carry the baby."
She handed me the baby, Lord.
"His name is Nathan," she said proudly.
"He's our first."
As soon as he was in my arms, Nathan stopped crying.
The young mother looked at me,
And there was admiration in her eyes, Lord.
It made me feel good all over.
"He's never taken to anyone like that," she told me.
"You have a way with babies.

I guess it's because you were a mother, too."
We walked to the store together, Lord,
And in no time Nathan was relaxed against my shoulder.
It felt good to have a baby in my arms again, Lord.
I've had my own, of course, and grandchildren, too.
But none of them are babies now.
I hummed softly to him,
And when Nathan fell asleep, I still held him.
His long lashes looked so beautiful against his tiny face.
When the girl had found just the right gift,
And we were ready to go,
We put Nathan back into his stroller.
He did not wake up.
And this time I pushed him.
I invited the mother for coffee,
And as we sat together in the booth,
She thanked me.
"I knew you'd know just what to do," she admitted.
"That's why I stopped in front of you.
I wanted someone who was old enough to know how to take
    care of Nathan."
I smiled at her.
"You'll learn quickly," I told her.
"Enjoy Nathan while he's small;
They grow up very fast."
"I will," she promised,
And I knew she meant it.
She thanked me again when we left each other, Lord,
And I never did find out her name.
But as she walked away, I felt warm inside.
My age and experience had showed, Lord.
They had served to help someone.
I walked straighter when I left the mall.
Thank you, Lord, for age and experience
And the chance to use them to help others.

Her Husband's Crying, Lord

Lord, I'm praying for my friend Ruth today,
And for her husband.
She told me that Bruce is crying again, Lord.
Until a month ago she had only seen him cry twice:
When his mother died
And when he fell from the tree and broke his leg in two places.
Now he is crying because of something else.
A month ago Bruce lost his job.
Ruth told me how slowly he walked into the house that night.
She said his shoulders were bent like an old man's.
She knew that what he had feared had happened.
"I'm out," Bruce told her, and he began to cry.
Ruth sat with him and held his hand,
Letting him cry.
She cried then, too, Lord,
But she was more angry than sorrowful.
What right did the company have to fire Bruce? she asked.
He had worked for them for almost twenty years—
The best years of his life.
He had done everything they asked of him.
He was loyal and hardworking.
He loved his work.
But Bruce is not young anymore,
And there had to be cutbacks.
He knew his department might be closed down.
The firing was not personal, the company told him;
He was just in an area that they no longer needed.
They would give him recommendations and severance pay.
"What will I do?" Bruce asked Ruth that day.

"What will we do?" he worried.

Ruth told him, "We'll get along just fine,"

And she hoped her voice sounded cheerful and confident.

"You'll get another job in a couple of weeks."

That was a month ago, Lord,

And there has been no new job for him.

Ruth and Bruce are our age—

An awkward age, it seems—

Too young to retire

But too old to be wanted in a new job.

Retirement brings recognition and thanks;

Being fired brings only hurt and rejection.

At first Bruce went out every morning to look for something
 new.

Ruth told me they mailed fifty résumés

To everyone and anyone they thought might have a lead
 for them.

No one needs a man Bruce's age to do what he can do.

He applied for unemployment compensation,

An embarrassment for him, Ruth said,

Not only on that first day when he applied,

But every time he goes for his check.

Bruce hates knowing that everyone knows he was fired,

That he is taking a "handout."

Ruth tried to tell him that he had paid into the funds

And that now he was entitled to take out of them.

It didn't help.

Bruce's pride was hurt repeatedly.

It's a pain that doesn't go away easily, Lord.

The biggest blow to his pride has been their financial status.

Ruth's part-time job has to become a full-time one.

Bruce was always proud that she did not have to work;

Her part-time job had been something she enjoyed.

Bruce knows Ruth is taking this new job, not because she
 wants to

Or because she likes the work,

But because they need the money to live on.

She has tried to tell him that it won't be long until he's working
   again,
But he doesn't believe her.
He doesn't know where to look, Lord.
He's gone everywhere, hat in hand.
Lord, give Bruce the faith that You have something better in
   store,
A job he will like and be good at.
Until then, Lord, help Ruth to help him.
She doesn't know what to say to him anymore
Or what to do.
Show her, Lord.
Bruce will have to be at home for a while
While Ruth works outside the house.
Help Bruce to see that keeping the house clean,
Washing the clothes,
And cooking the meals,
Are as important when he does them as when she did them
And he brought home the paycheck.
Help Ruth to show him that she loves him as much as ever
And respects him as much as before.
Help Bruce to understand that he is still useful
And that a man's worth is not measured by the work he does
Or the money he makes.
Make Bruce know he still counts, Lord,
To You and to the world.
Lord, if there's a job out there for Bruce,
Please let him find it soon.
You told us to come to You when we are heavy laden,
And I am heavy laden today for Ruth and Bruce.
Increase their faith in You and Your will for them.
Show them what to do next.
Show my husband and me what we can do to help them, too,
   Lord,
In a way that is friendly and not degrading or demanding.
Help us all to remember that this hard time will pass for them
But that You will not pass away—

Nor will we or they
If we keep our hearts and eyes on You.
Keep their faith and ours strong, Lord,
And lead us and them in the way You want us to go.

I'm Trying to Stay Modern, Lord

We are visiting in our son's home now, Lord.
    They make us feel so welcome when we come.
It's hard for them to get away long enough to travel
    as far as our home,
Even for the holidays.
So we do the traveling.
We are free to come and go as we want.
Letters, photos, and phone calls help keep a family close,
But nothing can compare to being together in person.
One thing I enjoy about visiting here for a few days
Is getting caught up on what's happening
In the modern world of the young.
Our granddaughter has a computer, Lord,
And she talks casually of bytes, floppy disks, and dot
    matrices.
She doesn't realize that I have no idea what she means!
Today, though, she suddenly understood that a computer was
    strange to me.
"I'll show you, Grandma," she promised.
And she did.
It was fascinating.
I remember when I bought my first electric typewriter;
I was sure I would never learn to use it.
My granddaughter's generation can skip it completely!
Children use computers in first grade,
And know exactly what their machines can do,
And how to make them do it.
I learned more quickly than I expected, Lord.
I've never been good at mechanical things.
But she was patient with me,

And almost as proud as I was when I finally "got it."
I think about all I have seen in my lifetime, Lord,
And all the things I remember my mother
And grandmother telling me about their younger days.
I want to tell my grandchildren how it was
"Back in the olden days."
I thank You that I can keep up with what is happening now,
And sometimes I wish I could live another hundred years
Just so I could see what is coming.
But that is not your plan, Lord,
And now my grandchildren are my teachers
As much as I am theirs.
I went shopping with my granddaughter, too, Lord,
And she showed me what her generation wears.
She laughed when I blushed at some of the T-shirts,
But I noticed that her face was a little bit pink, too.
She insisted I try on some of the clothes,
And then was kind enough to say I looked all right.

I know that some women of my generation dress like teens or
    preteens,
But I don't feel any need to pretend I am young.
I am content to know which designers are "in" for my grand-
    children,
And what their peers are wearing.
I like to hear the latest slang,
Even though I have to ask for a translation sometimes.
Common words mean completely different things now!
It reminds me of the days when my parents' patience was tried
    with my speech.
Some things never change, do they, Lord?
I learn who today's heroes and heroines are, too.
Even though my granddaughter may not always be a fan
    herself,
She knows who is riding the crest of popularity now.
I ask questions,
And she answers them.
I think the old must ask questions of the young.
There has to be a bridge over the generation gap,
And we can be it.
Thank You for this continuation, Lord.
I look forward to watching my "seed" continue
For as long as You give me, Lord.
It is Your promise to each generation.

Our Nest Is Empty Now, Lord

We left our "baby" on a doorstep today, Lord.
Oh, not as a foundling, but as a college freshman.
I felt as though I was abandoning her, though . . .
Or that she was abandoning me.
She was so eager for us to leave so she could get on with
   her adventure.
She's our baby, the last of our three to leave home.
I worry about her already, Lord.
Worrying is nothing new for me, but before I was close if she
   needed help.
Now I will be three hundred miles away.
We have tried to teach her, Lord, and we gave her to You when
   she was born.
She has not left You, Lord, and now I pray You will not
   leave her.
Give her the extra measure of assurance she will need this year.
Keep her faith strong when peer pressure tempts her to
   abandon her beliefs.
Lead her into the career You want her to follow.
Be with her as she dates more seriously and finally chooses
   her husband.
She is in Your hands, Lord.
Now my husband and I are home alone.
The house echoed with silence as we came in.
There was no loud music;
There was no ringing telephone;
There were no slamming doors.
We are really alone now, Lord.
We have made jokes about being able to get into the bathroom

Without a quarter hour's wait.
We have speculated about our savings at the grocery store.
But we both know we are talking to keep from crying.
Did You feel this way when You left Your disciples, Lord?
Did you wish that the years with them had not gone by so fast?
My friends warn me that I will have to find something to do
    with my time.
They talk of my going to college myself . . .
Or getting a full-time job instead of a part-time one . . .
Or being a volunteer for the church or a charity.
I know they are right, Lord.
I have seen too many women my age who live only
    in memories
Or for the brief times their children come home on holidays.
There is nothing new in their lives.
I don't want to be like that,
So I may try some new endeavors.
But right now I look at my husband,
And I know he is hurting as much as I am.
For years we have lived together
And raised our family together.
We've worked and planned and scheduled around
    the children,
And in doing that we grew apart without realizing it.
Now we must go back . . .
Back to when there was only the two of us.
I must learn to cook his favorite foods more often
And to talk about his interests.
We must begin again to grow together through common
    interests and hobbies.
Somehow we lost that during the hustle and bustle of
    raising children.
We are starting the second half of our lives, Lord.
It will be different in many ways from the first half,
Just as being a parent differed from being a child.
But in the most important way life will not change.
You have not left us, Lord.

You will be with us through this time the experts call the "empty
    nest" years.
You will be with us to help us learn to enjoy these years
And to let our children, even our "baby," go their own ways
And live their own lives.
It will be a new time with new images for all of us, Lord.
The house will seem too big and too quiet for a while,
Yet I know everything is all right
Because this is the way You have planned it.
I remember what You told Your disciples before You left them,
". . .I will be with you always, to the very end of the age."*
My life will never be quite the same again, Lord,
But there are many happy times coming
With different ways of enjoying life and You.
I'm looking forward to tomorrow, Lord . . .
And my new image on the other side of life.

*John 11:25

She's Always Been Alone, Lord

I had lunch with Martha today, Lord.
You know she's never married,
And she's always been alone.
We've been friends for years,
But this is the first time we've ever really talked about
    her situation
And about how we each feel in this last half of our very
    different lives.
"I used to envy you and the others," Martha said.
"You had bridal showers, weddings, and babies.
Sometimes I even envied you when the babies were sick
And you had to miss parties and things."
I nodded.
Bridal showers and weddings are fun.
Having a baby of your own to hold is a thrill.
But I had envied Martha, too, Lord.
"You were always doing exciting things," I told her.
"You always looked neat, confident, and important.
Sometimes I felt like a poor relation when I was with you.
And now you're an important person in your company,
Making decisions and policies.
Everyone respects you.
I envied you when I had to stay home with a sick child,
But you didn't have to worry about sitters or not going."
We can laugh at ourselves now, Lord,
Because we are older and wiser.
We agreed that You had given both of us much, Lord,
Even though You gave us different kinds of lives
And gifts to be used in different ways.

"I always had options," Martha went on.
"I could do what I wanted without having to consider anyone
   else's schedule.
I could decorate my apartment any way I wanted.
I could watch whatever TV programs I wanted.
I could go to bed and get up when I chose
And eat what and when it pleased me.
I could even change apartments or jobs
Without thinking about the effect on anyone else.
You were committed to sharing those decisions with
   a husband.
And without a husband to lean on,
I leaned on the Lord.
I could spend more time in prayer and Bible reading than you
   could.
And I have felt very close to the Lord all my life."
Then Martha and I talked about how we felt today.
We agreed we have mellowed a bit over the years.

We are not as quick to take offense at another's words
    or actions.
We are not as easily hurt.
We feel more sympathy for those who are hurting
And are quicker to try to help.
"I haven't envied you and the others for a long time,"
    Martha said.
"And now sometimes I feel a little sorry for you.
You will face problems I don't have to face
And some pains I won't feel.
I have no husband to lose;
No major adjustments to make.
I am still responsible only for myself,
And I can make plans now for when I am truly old
So that I will not have to worry about being cared for
    by others.
I will be able to adjust to those changes more easily than you
    will."
I don't know if she is right or wrong, Lord,
About who will adjust more easily.
I believe those who adjust best
Are those who walk close to You
And look for Your leading in everything.
But I know Martha feels confident, Lord,
And believes she has had the better life, all things considered.
We parted with a kiss,
And we agreed we will get together more often now.
As we walked away from each other,
I am sure we both thanked You
For our lives and the roads we took.
I would not trade places with Martha;
She would not trade with me.
We are both happy, Lord,
And content with what has gone before
And with what is to come.
Thank You, Lord, for caring for us all,
No matter how different our lives have been so far.

She's My Mother, Lord

She's my mother, Lord. She's seventy-eight years old,
And today I took her to a nursing home.
I thought of so many things, Lord.
I remember the cookies she baked for us for so many years.
Now she isn't allowed to eat any sweets at all.
I remember the dresses she sewed for me when I was young.
Now it takes her an hour to dress herself,
And then some of the buttons are in the wrong holes.
I know that for many people seventy-eight is still young,
But not for my mother, Lord.
She was able to stay in her own home until now.
I did her laundry with my family's.
I cleaned her house and did her shopping.
I was grateful to You to live close to her.
I'm the only child who does.
But a week ago she fell.
The doctor said she could not stay alone any more.
Mother and I had talked about nursing homes before.
She always said she did not want to live with her children
Or be a burden to anyone.
But we had never visited nursing homes.
I knew them only from friends' comments
And from what I could learn myself in a few days.
I felt so guilty there, Lord,
Going to strangers and asking about their care for my mother.
But I cannot take care of her.
She needs nursing, and I'm not a nurse.
She needs therapy to walk again,
And I'm not a therapist.

I tried to think of a way to keep her from a nursing home, Lord,
But I work at a full-time job
Now that we have two children in college.
I could not quit that job, Lord.
Our house is small, too.
There would be no privacy for my husband and me if Mother
    moved in.
There would be none for Mother, either.
She would know she was crowding us
And be sorry.
I know in my mind that there is no option except
    the nursing home.
Yet I feel so guilty turning her over to others.
She cared for me when I was young and could not care
    for myself.
Now I feel that I'm letting her down because I can't take care
    of her when she is the child.
What should I do, Lord?
What would You do?
I have just read from Your Word, Lord,
From John 19:26 and 27,
About how You died on the cross.
I have read this a thousand times, I'm sure,
And heard sermons on Your "seven last words" every
    Good Friday for years.
I've heard them sung and seen them performed in
    Passion plays.
Yet today, for the first time, I really understood the words
"Dear woman, here is your son . . ."
And "Here is your Mother."
You were dying, Lord.
You could no longer take care of Your mother on earth,
But You still loved her.
So You did the only thing You could do . . .
You turned her over to someone who could care for her.
Her care was first in Your mind.
I thank You for Your example, Lord.

As I read this, I know my guilty feelings are wrong.
I have done what is best for my mother, Lord,
Just as You did what You knew was best for Yours.
I have been too concerned about what others might think of me
    for putting my mother in a "home."
I will always wish it could have been different, Lord,
But I will try not to feel guilty.
I will visit my mother often.
I will bring her to our home for dinner
And for all our special occasions.
I will keep her a close part of our family,
Even though she must live apart from us.
I will let her keep her pride
And the knowledge that she is not a burden to anyone.
I will always love my mother, Lord . . .
And show it by my words and actions to her.

Help Her Make It Alone, Lord

My friend Lois called before breakfast, Lord.
Her husband died last night.
A heart attack.
I said what I pray were helpful words, Lord,
And went to stay with her until her children came.
I haven't been able to stop thinking about her today.
She's the first among my friends to be left alone.
I can't say the word "widow" yet, Lord.
I had never really thought about marriages ending that way.
"Until death do us part" is only a phrase when you're young,
But now we are no longer young.
We all know that marriages end this way.
I thought about my husband,
Who is still so strong and active,
And about me.
We have lived almost two-thirds of our lives together, Lord;
It's hard to remember life without him being here.
Yet one of us will eventually have to leave the other,
And statistics say I'll be the one left alone.
"He went quickly," Lois told me.
"He didn't have any pain."
I know she was trying to find something to comfort herself,
And it does comfort her, Lord.
I kissed my husband after I hung up the phone.
I'm grateful that we, too, have the kind of marriage
That won't need deathbed good-bye scenes.
Both of us would hate lingering, Lord,
Needing help to dress, to eat, to move,
Or not knowing the people who love us when they come.

Lois has gone through the funeral arrangements in a daze.
I watched her at the funeral home tonight,
Answering questions,
Explaining how it happened,
Thanking people for coming,
And smiling though her eyes were red.
Give her strength, Lord.
She has bolstered her children with her faith,
Remembering that while she has lost a husband,
They have lost a father.
Help me to remember that, too, Lord,
If my time comes to be alone.
When my husband and I went to bed tonight,
I thought of Lois.
Her bed must seem so big to her now,
And the house will be so empty and quiet in a few days.
People come now to help,
But they have their own lives that will keep them busy.
Lois will be on her own then.
She will turn on the TV just for the sound of human voices,
Not caring what the actors are doing on the screen.
She may even eat in front of it
To keep from sitting at the table that she once shared with her
    husband.
I thought of the details of life that a husband takes care of,
    Lord;
Things a woman alone has to learn to do for herself.
Lois doesn't know when their property tax is due
Or when to take the car for an oil change.
I'm sure she can't start the lawn mower alone.
Would I be able to learn so much so fast, Lord?
There will be many legal details, too.
Most of us don't know enough about our family finances.
We should have learned early in marriage,
But most of us didn't.
I opened our bedroom closet tonight
And saw all my husband's clothes hanging next to mine.

One of us will have to clean half of that closet someday,
    I realized.
Help that one to face that time with faith in You, Lord,
And faith in Your promise that
"He who believes in me will live,
Even though he dies." *
Help Lois to go on with her life, Lord;
Her husband would not want her to stop living.
Show Lois how to pick up the pieces
And go on with her life.
Help me and my husband to help her,
But not to smother her.
Help us to be there when she needs us
And to anticipate when those times will be
So that we can make the first move to comfort her.
I don't want to think about being alone, Lord.
Help me to be a good wife for as many more years as You
    give us.
And if I should be the one left to live alone,
Help me to keep busy with things that count,
Things that help others.
Show me such things to suggest to Lois,
Things that don't just keep her busy,
Such as joining a club she doesn't care about
Or going on trips to places she doesn't want to see,
But things that will broaden her interests and encourage
    friendships.
Give her the strength to visit his grave, Lord,
But only now and then,
Because he's not really there.
I especially thank You tonight, Lord,
For the years my husband and I have had together.
I am sad, thinking about the end of those years.
My friend's sorrow has prompted such thoughts,
But I am not worried, Lord.
I know that when the time comes,
You will help whichever one of us is left alone

To go on living with and for You.
Please give that same strength to Lois, Lord,
Now and for the rest of her life, day by day.
Give it, too, to all the others who have been left alone by death
And who live with happy memories.

*Matthew 28:20

Timmy's Special, Lord

I just came from a women's meeting at church, Lord,
And I am depressed.
One of our new members told about a cute thing
  her grandson did.
He is the same age as our grandson, Timmy.
Then she brought out pictures.
The other women did the same thing.
Everyone our age has grandchildren, Lord,
And everyone is proud of them.
When I made no move to show pictures,
The new woman asked if I had grandchildren.
There was an awkward silence, Lord.
I wanted to shout at her, "Yes! Oh, yes!
But he's mentally retarded!
He'll never do the clever things your grandchildren do.
He'll never be able to do more than routine work.
He may die young."
The others knew what I was thinking.
Someone quickly changed the subject.
I do have pictures of Timmy, Lord,
But it embarrasses people to see them.
So I don't show them.
I look at them, though—often.
As You know, I pray for Timmy every day.
I write him little notes . . .
Notes I know he may never understand.
I send him brightly colored pictures to hang on his wall,
And I send him shirts and pajamas with animals on them.
When Timmy was first born, I was angry with You, Lord.

How could You have let this happen to us?

We had all wanted this child so much.

No one on either side of the family has ever been mentally retarded.

I was embarrassed by Timmy, too, Lord.

I can admit that now, although I couldn't at first.

"What will people think?" I worried.

I quickly learned that those who love us will sympathize
   with us,
And love Timmy as he is.
Those who don't love us will usually avoid us when Timmy
   is visiting;
They may avoid talking about grandchildren or retarded
   children when we're around.
And I understand that, Lord, even when I'm hurting.
Timmy's parents accepted him sooner than I did, Lord.
They knew right away that Timmy was special
And that You had given him to them to be special parents.
Did You make me his grandmother because I'm a special
   person, Lord?
I'd like to think that You did.
I remember the story of the children coming to You, Lord,
How You welcomed them and told Your disciples
That of such are the kingdom of Heaven.
I wonder if there were any retarded or handicapped children in
   that group.
In the pictures I've seen, the artists do not show any.
They drew only healthy, alert children around You.
Yet there must have been some there like Timmy,
Or some who were crippled or deaf or blind.
They would have wanted to see You, too, Lord.
And you loved them just as much as You loved the normal
   children.
It still hurts when others show pictures of perfect
   grandchildren
And tell of the intelligent things they do
Or of their artistic and athletic achievements.
But someday I know you will take away all my hurt,
Just as You have taken much of it away already.
And if someday I am the grandmother of many normal
   children,
I will not forget Timmy, the special one.
Timmy will always have his own place in my heart, Lord . . .
A big place because he needs it very much.

Thank You for My New Freedoms, Lord

I woke up with a strange sense of freedom today, Lord.
As I thought about why I felt this way,
I knew it was because I am no longer young
And tied to the many demands youth has on freedom.
Now that my husband and I are older, Lord,
We are free of the demands of others' time;
Free to do what we want.
When our children were home, we were always busy
Keeping up with their schedules.
We drove them to and from meetings, lessons, and practices.
This was not a burden, Lord;
It was a privilege we enjoyed.
It gave us time to be alone with our children,
And a chance to meet new friends
As we waited with other parents for the children to appear.
Now we have time to do what we want to do.
I have time to read all those books I have wanted to read over
   the years,
Even the long epics.
My husband has begun reading all the works of a single writer,
One whose writing and lifestyle he admires.
A friend our age is building furniture in his basement;
Another is making a quilt.
We all agree, Lord,
That there still isn't time to do all we want to.
Time is a wonderful gift from You, Lord,
And I thank you for it.
There's a freedom with money now, too, Lord,
That wasn't there in our early years of marriage.

Then we had to watch every penny
And save for the future.
Now the future is here,
And we can enjoy it.
We can go out to dinner now and then,
Especially to restaurants with senior citizens prices.
We can buy things for ourselves or others
When we want to.
We don't overspend, Lord;
Our habits are too ingrained.
But we are enjoying this new freedom.
We can give more to those who work for You, Lord,
In other countries or within our own society.
I realize that my freedom has another side, too, Lord.
I may be free to do more of what I want to do,
But now I'm also free to NOT do what I don't really want to.
When I was young, I thought I had to say yes to every request,
Whether it was baking chocolate chip cookies for a Cub Scout
    meeting,
Having a garage sale the same day my neighbors did,
Or reading a book because it was on the best-seller list.
I thought people would not like me if I did not go along.
Now, at my age, I don't worry about whether everyone likes
    me or not.
I am secure about myself.
I know a few people will not like me,
And certainly not everyone will want me for a best friend.
Now I find it easier to say no
To things I know I am not qualified for
Or things I don't care about doing.
I don't keep my house quite as neat,
Or have the floors as spotless, either.
Instead I enjoy my home and husband.
I used to think I had to keep up with my friends;
Now I know differently.
I am myself;
They are themselves.

At our age we can say, "Vive la difference,"
And respect what the other is and does.
I have another kind of freedom, Lord,
That comes with age.
It's a freedom from so many doubts about You.
When I was young, it was hard to have faith sometimes.
Now I have lived long enough to say with the psalmist,
"I was young and now I am old,
Yet I have never seen the righteous forsaken . . . ."*
Oh, I still have questions,
And I will have them until I see You face to face.
But my faith is stronger now than when I was young.
I read Psalm 92 this morning, Lord.
Verses 14 and 15 spoke out to me.
You have promised that we shall bear fruit in our old age,
And I want to do that, Lord.
I want to do the things I do best
And help someone as I do them.
Give me the grace to carry through my projects, Lord,
And the wisdom to choose them.

*Psalm 37:25

He Hears a Different Drummer, Lord

He's asleep in his old bed upstairs, Lord,
Our son who is several years past the legal voting age.
He came home last night, looking depressed and"down."
He stood in the living room, a small bag at his feet.
"I got laid off," he said.
His voice was low, and he didn't look at his father and me.
He's been laid off before, Lord. Twice. And he's quit jobs twice,
    too.
It's not that he's a poor worker, Lord,
Or dumb.
He was in the top third of his high school class, but he didn't
    want college.
"I've had enough school," he said. "I want to live."
We went along with his first menial job,
Trying not to compare him to his friends in college.
He quit that job and went on to something else,
And then to something else.
When the layoffs start, he is "last hired, first fired."
And now he's home again, looking like a failure to the world.
His dream now, he says, is to have his own business.
He has the ideas and the plans,
But I don't know if he can do it, Lord.
It's such a big world to tackle alone,
And businesses fail so quickly today.
We have tried to help him before, Lord.
We have loaned him money, which he has always repaid,
And our home has always been open to his return.
Were we wrong, Lord? Some of our friends say so.
They think we should let him sink or swim on his own.

Sometimes they hint that his failures are the result of mistakes
    that we made when he was young.
All parents make mistakes, Lord,
And we treated him the way we did the others.
We had no trouble as he grew up.
He seems a lot like the prodigal son you told us about, Lord.
He has gone his own way,
Looking for his own goals.
He has not squandered our wealth,
But he has lived in a single tiny room that made me shudder.
He has skipped meals and had an empty refrigerator
Until we came with bags of groceries.
Our other children are upset with him, too,
Like the prodigal son's older brother.
This brother is an embarrassment to them;
None of their friends have brothers who are "unsuccessful,"
Brothers who live different lifestyles
And seem to fail at each new thing.
When our friends learn that he's home again, they will
    look away.
Their children this age are settled in their work and lives.
Their sons and daughters are "successful."
But we're his parents, Lord, and we love him.
We will help him again this time, however we can.
I pray that You will lead him.
I pray that You will show us how to help him to do well
    this time.
I remember him as a small boy, Lord, and I thank You for
    those years.
He was the most loving of our children,
The first one to laugh at everything.
Our son hears a different drummer, Lord,
Just as You did.
You did not do things the way people thought You should.
You did what You knew was right for You,
Fulfilling God's plan for salvation.
It must have hurt Your mother to see You laughed at,

To hear others say You were demented, or a glutton, or a
  drunkard,
To finally watch You crucified as a common criminal.
Yet she knew that You did what was right for You.
Help me to see that what our son does will eventually be right
  for him—
Oh, maybe not yet, although I pray it will be soon,
But someday.
Help me to be proud of him as though he were "successful" in
  the world's eyes.
Help me to remember he is an individual—a child of God.
Help me to encourage him, Lord,
To find his own place, his own responsibility,
Regardless of what others think and say.
It's not easy having him home again, Lord.
We were just getting used to the advantages of being alone.
Help me to know when to tell him, "Enough,"
And when to hold him close as though he were still a child.
Help me to turn a deaf ear to the comments of my friends,
And never to compare him with others,
Either in this family or another.
On the other hand, Lord, don't let me get so involved with his
  problems
That I can't live my own life.
I'm an individual, too, and must do what is right for me.
You will show me how to act and react, Lord,
And I will lean on You through all of this.
Thank You for being here when we need You, Lord,
And for giving us this son who hears a different drummer.

I'm a Mother-in-Law, Lord

I'm a mother-in-law, Lord.
Just saying it makes me feel older.
Of course, it didn't happen overnight,
But now it is final.
The wedding service changed many lives, Lord,
In ways we have not yet started to know or understand.
I have never been a mother-in-law before,
Although I hope to be again.
I used to laugh at mother-in-law jokes.
Now I cringe
Because it's me they're laughing at.
Are the jokes really true, Lord?
Some of my friends think so.
They say my daughter-in-law is my enemy because we love the
    same man.
But if we both love him, Lord,
Don't we both want him to be happy?
Aren't our aims the same even if our methods are different?
I love my new daughter-in-law, Lord,
And I think she loves me, too.
Yet, we are both shy and nervous when we're together.
I want to be a good mother-in-law, Lord—
One like Naomi was to Ruth.
I used to read that story and see myself as Ruth;
Now I am Naomi, and I must trust You as she did.
Give me the faith and heart of Naomi, Lord.
Help me to remember that I am the mature one,
The one with years of living and experience behind me.
If we have disagreements,

I'm the one who should take the first step to bring back
   harmony and peace.
I pray that we won't have those kinds of differences,
But if we do, give me the bigness of spirit to apologize first.
Help me to remember how it was when I was first married
And wanted to do everything myself and in my own way.
How I wanted to prove I was capable at everything I did!
I hated to be told that something would not work
Or that there was a better way to do it.
Help me not to be critical when I see her doing things
   differently
And to remember that I may bother her sometimes, too.
Help me to remember, Lord, that although I love him as much
   as ever,
My son is no longer all mine.
I do not have to be responsible for his clean shirts
Or hot dinners.
Now I can simply enjoy his company
As one adult to another—
The way I have always enjoyed the company of my friends.

Some tell me that my son will never be mine again,
But I don't want him to be.
This is why I raised him;
He is now an independent and mature adult.
Help me to remember that certain things are private, Lord,
Things a husband and wife alone should share—
How much money they have,
How they spend it,
And their special times alone together.
Let me bite my tongue before I ask questions
Whose answers are none of my business.
Help me to know when to offer my help
And when to let them struggle on their own.
Let me remember that although I'm her husband's mother,
I am not my daughter-in-law's real mother.
Help me to step back and give her mother her rightful place.
Make me understand why she will always love her own mother
    more than she loves me
And tell her own mother more than she tells me.
I would be thrilled if she were to call me "Mother" or "Mom,"
But if she doesn't,
Help me to understand that she wants that name reserved for
    her own mother,
And to accept whatever names she wants to call me.
Bless this new family, Lord,
This couple that is in love
And eager to please each other and to grow together.
Keep them together, Lord, through good times and bad,
Remembering their wedding vows and working to live up
    to them.
Turn them to You, Lord,
So that You will be the foundation of their home.
Bless the children they will have some day,
And help my son and daughter-in-law to be good parents,
    Lord.
Thank You for bringing this couple together
And for making me a mother-in-law.

Do I Have to Love Them as Much as My Own, Lord?

My daughter is being married, Lord,
To a man who already has two children.
He is a fine Christian, Lord,
And the children are happy, well-behaved, and beautiful.
But they are not mine, Lord.
They have other grandparents—real ones,
Not ones they have picked up through a second marriage.
They are the same ages as my grandchildren,
And I compare them.
I know I shouldn't do that, Lord, but I can't seem to help it.
I compare them,
And I want my own to look better.
I want those of my own blood to be smarter, more gifted,
    and bigger.
When they are all here together, I try hard to be fair.
I count the cookies carefully so that no one gets more than his
    or her share.
I make them take turns on the swing or the tricycle.
Sometimes I let my stepgrandchildren go first;
Sometimes I take their side in an argument,
As though I favor them more than my own.
Yet I don't.
I do it because I feel guilty for not loving these new children in
    the family.
What can I do, Lord?
I don't want to feel this way,
I'm almost sure it's wrong.
Yet I can't help it.
Do I really have to love them as much as my very own, blood-

related grandchildren?
Do I have to want them around as much as my own?
Do I have to keep as many pictures of them in my wallet?
Or in the living room?
Do I have to, Lord?
I know I have to treat them the same way I do my own,
And I can do this.
I can spend the same amount for their birthday and Christmas
    gifts;
I can give them the same treats when they visit.
I can take them on as many outings.
But that's not the same as love, Lord.
You don't say anything in Your Word about grandparents,
    Lord.
I've searched.
So I ask You to lead me personally.
I am afraid my own grandchildren will begin to feel slighted.
My stepgrandchildren have other grandparents who love them
And who will do things for and with them.
Mine will not get as many presents,
Nor have as many sets of grandparents to visit.
At least this is what I tell myself, Lord.
Yet if I don't treat my stepgrandchildren equally,
How will they feel deep inside?
Will they see my favoritism?
Will they think they have done something wrong—
Something for which I am punishing them?
How will their father feel?
Will he want to come to visit less often?
Will he begin to hate me because of what I feel toward
    his children?
And what about their new mother, my daughter?
Will she feel that she has to choose between her husband and
    me—
Not permanently, of course,
But on Sunday afternoons, perhaps?
Lord, help me to love those children who are not really mine.

Help me to help my daughter to love them, too,
Help me to do the right things to be an example for her,
Even if at first I do them for the wrong reasons.
That's how love grows, isn't it, Lord?
You act like you love,
And eventually you do.
I will try harder, Lord, to show love to these children.
I will try harder to show love to my own grandchildren, too.
But I will need lots of help from You.
I will need Your help every day.
I will start by praying for all my grandchildren, Lord,
The ones who are related by blood and the ones who are
    related by marriage.
Bless them all, Lord, and lead them in Your way.
Keep them safe as they play and grow;
Keep them close to You through their lives.
And help my stepgrandchildren to see that I want to love them,
    Lord,
And that I want them to love me.
Then we will be one family—
The way You want us to be.

Solomon Should Have Known Grandparents, Lord

I 've just reread the story of Solomon, Lord,
How he ordered the baby cut in two
So that each mother could have half.
It was a wise decision.
The real mother stepped forward to give up the child
To save it from death.
But how would Solomon have dealt with grandparents, Lord?
We cannot afford to spend as much on gifts and treats
As our grandchildren's other grandparents can.
We cannot afford to take them to faraway theme parks
Or to professional sporting events.
We cannot afford the stereos and minibikes
Or the clothes with the designer labels.
When I see what the other grandparents have done for them,
I can understand why the children prefer to visit there instead
    of here.
But we should not have to "buy" our grandchildren's love.
Should we?
Yet to children "things" are very important—
The right animal on their shirts,
The "in" style of everything.
What should we do, Lord?
Should we enter the competition?
We could sacrifice some other things, I'm sure,
But it doesn't seem right.
Should I talk to the other grandparents?
What would I say?
They can easily afford what they are giving to their
    grandchildren.

Would it be right to ask them to stop giving so much
Just because we can't?
Should I talk to my own children—
Explain how we love the grandchildren but can't afford some
    things?
Would it embarrass them?
Would it make them think less of us
Or of themselves?
I don't know what to do, Lord.
Please help me to know how to act when our gifts
    look so small.

I have read in Your Word again, Lord,
What the apostle Paul said about love.
I had lost sight of what real love is—
Love for grandchildren, too, Lord.
I have let myself envy.

I have let myself be proud and self-seeking.
I have let myself keep a record of the wrongs done by those
who have more money than we have.

Forgive me, Lord.
I will try to remember what real love is.
I will try to make my love for my grandchildren that kind of
love.
If we cannot give expensive gifts,
I will spend more time in selecting them
To be sure each gift is "just right" for the one receiving it.
I will spend more time in making things—
Like homemade cookies and popcorn balls.
I will try to be available, too, Lord,
For when they need someone just to talk to.
I will spend more time playing with my grandchildren
And reading to them
And helping with homework, if they ask me.
I will stop comparing our gifts for them
With their other grandparents' gifts.
We will give what we can
And give it with love.
My decision may not be as wise as Solomon's, Lord,
Because it will still hurt when I see gifts bigger and more
expensive
Than ours.
But I will try to remember what Paul said about real love,
And I will show that kind of love to my grandchildren in little
ways.
They may not understand now, Lord.
They may prefer the expensive gifts.
But someday they will realize that we were giving of ourselves
Rather than competing for their love or favor with monetary
things.
Then they, too, will know what real love is all about,
And we will have given more than we could buy—
We will have given them everything.

I'm Still Learning, Lord

I've started a new project today, Lord.
I am taking a course at our local college:
Chinese history.
China has fascinated me
Ever since I was a child and read about Hudson Taylor.
I never felt Your call to be a missionary,
But I felt a strong desire to give to Chinese missions.
Lately I've felt the pull of China again.
I hesitated to take the step to get into the class, Lord.
When I was in school years ago,
Women my age never thought of being students again.
I've read that many women are doing this now,
But the ones I have read about were much younger than I am.
When I was their age,
I did not have time to go to a class
And do the studying and the reading it would take.
I was too busy to even consider it.
We did not have the money to pay for such a frivolous thing,
     either.
Now, at my age, I have the time,
And we can afford the fees.
My husband encouraged me.
"If you want to do it, just do it!" he said.
So I went to the college and registered.
I wondered how it would feel to be older than most students'
     mothers.
I wondered how it would feel to be older than the professor!
I wondered if I could learn to study again.
I went into the class with my brand-new notebook,

50

My brand-new pens,
My brand-new textbook.
It was a small class, Lord,
And I was the oldest by far.
But the students did not act surprised to see me.
They nodded to me just as they did to the others they did not
    know.
And I found something out very quickly, Lord:
I knew more about China than anyone but the professor!
I have had the time to read about it;
I have been reading about China for years,
Years the younger students have not yet had.
I have also lived through times they have only read about,
Times that involved China and our country.
Oh, they have seen selected pictures of World War II
And highlights of the fighting in China,
But they have known only secondhand this period
And the true-life stories of those days.
I learned that I could easily follow the professor
And take my notes.
I even answered a question once, Lord!
After the class the professor smiled at me
And welcomed me.
He surprised me when he said,
"We all like to see older people in our classes.
They are serious students.
They usually get very good grades, too."
I almost floated out of the building, Lord,
And into the student union for a cup of coffee.
I was sitting alone at a table when two students from the class
    entered.
"May we sit with you?" one asked.
I couldn't believe it!
These young people wanted to sit with *me*.
And there were plenty of empty tables, too.
"Of course." I smiled at them.
We had a wonderful twenty minutes together, Lord.

They are Christians, too.
They are in love with each other,
With life, and with the future.
They are excited about the lives they are going to live.
At first I felt like their mother,
But that passed quickly.
We were all only students there.
We discussed the professor,
Wondering what kind of tests he will give
And whether he will require long papers.
I ended by inviting them to come to our church
And then home for dinner with us on Sunday.
They accepted with smiles and happiness.
Home-cooked meals don't come often in college.
I thank You, Lord, for leading me to this course at this time.
I thank You for giving me two new friends
And the maturity to help them.
The experience gave me self-confidence.
I may never have a chance to visit China, Lord,
Or to use the knowledge I'm getting,
But I remember the many times You spoke of wisdom and
    knowledge
In Your Word, Lord.
You said, "Wise men [and I know that means me, too] store up
    knowledge,"*
And, "The discerning heart seeks knowledge."**
That's what I am doing, Lord.
Now I've got to study.
I have to show that an old dog *can* learn new tricks!

*Proverbs 10:14

**Proverbs 15:14

What's to Become of Us, Lord?

I just came from seeing my grandchildren, Lord.
   I watched them playing on the swings
And building castles in the sandbox.
They were happy, laughing, secure.
They know they are loved;
They know they are cared for.
They cannot yet read the headlines in the newspapers
Or understand what they see on the six o'clock news.
But I can, Lord.
There is still starvation in Africa,
Harsh-sounding words from major capitals,
And testing of weapons everywhere.
The psalmist said that the earth is Yours, Lord—
And everything in it
And all who live in it.
But now we have the power to blow up Your world
And kill every living thing.
We know that war is only the touch of a button away.
You promised Noah that You would never destroy the world
   again with water, Lord;
You said nothing about an atomic war that we humans start.
What will happen to my grandchildren then, Lord?
Will they be adults, trying to shield their own children from
   the horror?
Will they have to suffer physical and mental pain?
And what if no war comes?
Will my grandchildren spend every hour of their lives
   fearing it?
What about the earth itself, Lord?

Will there be pure water for them to drink?
Will there be fuels to keep them warm?
Will there be enough food to maintain life?
Will there be trees, flowers, and grass for them to enjoy?
Or will they live in cramped, boxlike apartments
Because there are too many people?
Will they have to wear protective clothing and masks
To keep out the pollutants in the air?
Will they have to live in constant fear of radioactive waste
Or the breakdown of an atomic reactor?
Will they be able to fly to other countries, Lord,
Without fear of being taken hostage?
And what about the streets then?
Will they be safe to walk on—even in daylight?
Or will my grandchildren have to carry weapons
And travel in groups for protection?
I look at my grandchildren, Lord,
And wonder what life has in store for them.
There are so many things parents can't control or prevent

No matter how much they love their children.
Will my grandchildren face worldwide epidemics of diseases
    we don't even know about yet?
We didn't know about AIDS or sickle-cell anemia when I was
    their age.
What future illnesses do we know nothing about now?
I worry about the future of the world for this generation, Lord.
Then I remember Your words:
"Surely I will be with you always,
To the very end of the age."*
Perhaps my grandchildren will live to see
The end of the age, Lord.
But if they do, they will also live to claim Your promise:
"I will be with you always. . . ."
Every generation has faced serious problems, Lord.
Every generation has wondered if its children would grow up
To have children of their own before the world was destroyed.
The problems have been different, Lord;
War, even if not an atomic one, has always been a threat.
Yet some things get better as time goes by.
My children have never known a real depression, Lord,
Or the sight of a friend dying of tuberculosis
Or limping from polio.
I think about their future, Lord,
And I know that there is only one thing I can do for them.
I can put them in Your hands, under Your promise,
Just as my parents and grandparents put me there so many
    years ago.
Thank You, Lord, for that promise we can lean on
When we are afraid
Or in pain
Or caught in a situation about which we can do nothing.
It's enough for me, Lord—Your promise—
Enough to base my future on
And my grandchildren's future, too.
It's enough to give me peace of mind
And take away my fear of the years to come.

*Matthew 28:20

How Can I Make It A Home, Lord?

We have made the decision, Lord.
We are moving to an apartment.
We have discussed the pros and cons for months.
I know there are good reasons to do it now.
This house takes a lot more work
Than a four-room apartment will.
I won't have to take care of things such as cleaning the attic
Or washing the windows.
My husband won't have to mow the lawn in the summer
Or shovel snow in winter.
He won't have to fix faucets and doors and other things
When they break.
We'll make a single telephone call, and the repair will be made.
But this house has been home for a long time, Lord.
Our children grew up here.
They played in the yard;
They studied in their rooms; they entertained friends in the
    kitchen.
There are nicks in the woodwork
And worn places on the floor—
Imperfections that bring memories of happy times.
There will be no grilled hamburgers in an apartment
And no roller-skating in the basement.
There won't be room for a lot of our possessions, Lord.
We'll have to leave some old furniture behind for the sale;
And the things a mother keeps—
Cards from her children,
A clothespin recipe holder,
A ceramic trivet—

They will have to be packed away.
I don't really want to move, Lord.
I don't know how I can make those four rooms seem like home.
They are all painted the same neutral color.
The carpet was not worn by my family's feet,
But by the feet of strangers,
Many strangers.
Some of our things will come with us, of course,
But much of it will look out of place there.
The furniture will be too big
Or the wrong style
Or the wrong color.
Our children tell us that we can afford to buy new things that
    will fit there,
But I don't want new things, Lord.
There are no memories in new things.
There will be no memories in those rooms, either.
They will be like a sterile field.
Yet I know this move to a smaller place is best for us,
And I want to be cheerful and enthusiastic.
I want to look at it like a new adventure.
But I feel too old for an adventure like this, Lord.
Please, help me.
I remember that You once said You had no place to lay
    Your head.
How much better off we are than that, Lord!
We will still have our family,
Whether we live in an apartment or a house.
Our grandchildren may love the idea of sleeping on the floor
    there
Rather than in beds in the bigger house.
We will still have each other, Lord.
Some couples are not so fortunate.
Death has taken one of them;
The other must live alone.
Help me to see my blessings, Lord,
And not take them for granted.

Help me to remember that the size of my house is
    not important;
The love that lives there is.
I will do all I can to make the apartment feel like home
For my husband and me.
I will keep doing things the way I always have—
The cooking will taste the same;
The bookshelves will look the same.
Help me to remember that making a home is much more
    important
Than keeping up a house, Lord.
And You will be with us—
Welcome in our home
No matter what its size.

Why Can't I Do What I Used to Do, Lord?

I'm slowing down, Lord.
I hadn't realized it until today.
Yesterday was the day for a "deep cleaning" in the bedroom—
More than just a quick dusting and sweeping.
I've always been able to do it in one morning,
And that's what I planned to do this time.
But it didn't work out that way yesterday.
I found that the mattress and springs weighed a lot more than I
    remembered,
And they were more awkward to move and turn.
The closet was bigger, too,
With twice as many things in it as last year.
Even climbing the stepladder to take down the light fixture was
    more difficult than last year.
Did someone raise the ceiling
Or make the ladder steps further apart?
It was almost dinner time when I was through,
And I was so tired!
My husband understood,
And we went out for dinner.
I slept well last night, Lord,
But this morning I was stiff all over!
My back ached and my legs, too.
Exercising didn't help the way it usually does.
I've noticed, too, that I can't walk as far as I used to, Lord,
Or stay up as late—
Even for a good old movie on TV.
I've never really thought about old age, Lord.
Oh, I suppose I always expected that "some day"

I'd have gray hair
And wrinkles
And aches and pains.
But "some day" was not now!
Old age was for people my mother's age,
Not mine.
I don't know when I began slowing down, Lord,
Or how.
I look back and realize that it's been several years since I swam
     the length of the pool,
Or walked to the store and back;
Or climbed up on the cupboard to reach a shelf
Instead of getting the step stool.
I don't remember when that one gray hair
Became so many that they outnumbered the black ones;
Or when those wrinkles worked themselves so deeply into
     my face
Or when the veins began to show on the back of my hands.
When I go to the doctor for my checkups, he always says,
"You're looking good."
Then he spoils it by adding, "For your age."
Of course, he's only thirty, Lord.
Some say old age is the "golden" time, Lord,
While others say it's the worst of all times.
I suspect both ideas are partly right
And partly wrong.
There are many things I can't do anymore,
And probably more I won't be able to do in another fifteen or
     twenty years.
But there are advantages, too.
I have lived long enough to know how to avoid what I can't do,
To turn down invitations and temptations without
     embarrassment.
I have learned how to make life's rough places a little smoother.
Help me, Lord, not to wish for what is past,
But to look forward to what is to come.
Help me to keep myself in as good physical shape as I can

And to do all I can to always look my best.
Help me to use my experience and knowledge to help others,
If they will listen,
But not to force my ideas or opinions on them.
All generations and individuals must learn for themselves.
"Just give them time," I've heard people say,
"And they'll understand."
Thank You for the medical knowledge and remedies that hold
    off the pains of old age,
And help me to live a normal life for many more years.
Help me to accept the gray hair and wrinkles as signs of victory
Over the trials and obstacles of life,
And the aches and pains as simple inconveniences.
I don't want to be old, Lord,
At least not yet.
You were never old, Lord,
But surely You knew many old people
And sympathized with them
And loved them.
That's all I ask You to do for me, Lord—
Sympathize and love.
Then old age will not be painless,
But it will be glorious.

Why Do We Have to Move, Lord?

The company has transferred my husband, Lord,
Out of town, out of state, almost out of the country.
We must leave in six weeks.
Why do we have to move
At this time of our lives?
We have lived in this town for years.
We expected to retire here,
We have friends here,
And one of our children lives here.
We love this town, Lord,
And now the company says we have to leave it.
We don't really have much choice,
Although we have talked about options.
If we refuse to go, it will mean no raise,
And in the near future, possibly a demotion
Or early retirement.
My husband does not want any of these.
Actually, I think he wants to move, Lord.
I can sense his enthusiasm during our conversations.
The new responsibility excites him;
He thinks of the new title, the new work, the new life.
I can't help thinking about the old.
I don't want to have to find a new church, Lord;
Our present church is like a family to us.
I don't want to have to find new stores for shopping,
A new beauty parlor,
A new doctor and dentist,
New friends.
I am the one who will have to do all the "finding."

My husband will be too busy at his new assignment.
We are so comfortable here, Lord;
Everything is in its place for us.
Are we too comfortable?
Is that why we're having to move?
I have read the books on how to pack
And how to get settled in a new home.
We have gotten leads on some houses there, too.
Soon we will spend a few days in the new city to look at them.
My husband wants to go, Lord.
For his sake I will try to have a positive attitude.
I read the other day what Paul said about being content.
He said he had learned to be content in whatever state he
    was in.

I know he didn't mean Ohio or Illinois or California,
But for me that could be what You mean.
You are reminding me that I can be content anywhere
If I make up my mind to give the new place a chance,
If I work at getting acquainted with new people,
And if I remember that You are going with me.
Help me to remember this, Lord.
As I move into a strange house, a strange town, a strange state,
Help me to remember that there are good, friendly, helpful
    people everywhere
And that a stranger is just a friend you haven't met yet.
Let me remember that sometimes I must make the first move to
    get acquainted.
We will write ahead to our new church, Lord;
Our pastor here has given us the address.
We can start to get the weekly bulletins and newsletters
So that we will be familiar with some of the names before
    we arrive.
We can visit the church while we are house hunting.
We can start to get the local newspaper, too,
So that we will know what is happening before we move in.
I don't want to forget my old friends
And the happy times we've had in this town.
But I don't want to cling to the old—
Not when You have opened a new door for us.
I want to go forward,
Even when it hurts to leave the old behind;
Because if we don't go forward,
We stagnate.
Stagnation can be comfortable, Lord,
And it would be easy to refuse to move.
We would manage somehow if my husband had to retire early,
But we would not be growing.
Help me to remember all this
When I feel alone in the new town.
Help me to let You lead us
And to be content in whatever state I am.

What Will He Do All Day, Lord?

It's finally come, Lord—
The day my husband has known about for years:
His last day at work.
He's cleaned out his desk,
The accumulation of years,
And said his good-byes to people he has worked with for years.
The company gave him a dinner
And a plaque.
Tomorrow he will not have to get up at six o'clock.
He is planning to sleep late
And then to go fishing.
I don't know how he really feels about this retirement, Lord,
Not deep down inside.
He talks and acts as though he's happy about it,
But I can't help wondering if that's how he really feels.
And even if it is, I worry about what will happen when the
    newness wears off.
Right now retirement is like a vacation for him,
But this vacation will last the rest of his life.
My friends who have retired husbands tell me the worst things,
    Lord.
They say he will be "under my feet" all day,
That he will trail behind me as I do the housework,
That he will not want me to go to the store alone
Or even to visit a neighbor.
They say he will start to find fault with the way I do things in
    the kitchen
And in my other daily tasks.
They say he will rearrange the cupboards

And suggest new places to put the furniture,
New ways to clean and cook and plan.
They say that I will get tired of his always being here,
That I will find jobs for him to do outside or downtown.
I know this can happen, Lord,
But I don't want it to happen to us.
We have worked hard for many years to get to today,
And I don't want those years to be wasted
Because we can't handle being together all day.
When we were first married, we wanted to be together
    constantly.
We begrudged the time we had to go to our separate jobs;
We counted the hours until we were together again.
Now we will have all the hours together we want.
Will our mutual interests and activities fill those hours?
Will our relationship grow more meaningful?
Will our individuality suffer?
Will he miss the stimulation and challenge of his former
    career?
I need Your help, Lord.
Help me to be patient with him when he is bored.
Help me to remember that this is his home, too,
As much as it is mine.
Let me be willing to share my work with him,
Even though he wants to do it differently than I do.
Most of all, help me to be willing to change,
Willing to drop what I'm doing and go with him
When he wants to go out for coffee
Or on a picnic,
Or to a show.
Let me remember that the housework will always be here;
He and I won't be.
Help him, too, Lord,
To continue to feel important,
To know that even though he is not a wage earner anymore,
He is still a valuable, intelligent person.
He is still the same man he has always been.

Give us the insight to look at this as a second chance together—
A chance to do more of what we want to do
And less of what is required.
Give us both a sense of humor, Lord,
Because when we're together so much we will need it.
There will be times when we will argue
And perhaps even shout at each other.
Give us patience
When things do not go according to schedule or custom.
I am looking forward to these next years, Lord,
And I pray You will help us to make the most of them.
They will be a chance to serve You more,
If You will open the doors for us.
Lead us, Lord, as we go into this next phase of our lives.
Keep us as You have always kept us,
And give us Your peace.

My Child's Hurting and I Can't Fix Things, Lord

Our younger daughter called last night, Lord.
She and her husband are getting a divorce.
He has already moved out, she said.
She was crying, Lord, when she told us,
"He found someone else."
I know these things happen
More today than they did when we were first married,
But it is a shock when it's your child who is hurting.
When she was little I could make a hurt better with a kiss,
Or with a dab of medicated cream,
Or a fancy bandage.
I could help her with other hurts, too.
With my arms around her,
I assured her that missing the big party was not the end of
    the world.
She believed me then, Lord.
I knew at least some of the answers
Because I had lived through those problems myself.
But I have never had a husband leave me,
Never faced the prospect of lawyers, judges, and decrees
That would leave me alone.
I can't fix things for her now, Lord.
It looked like a good marriage—
As good as most and better than some.
They seemed right for each other then, Lord.
What happened?
When did it start to change for them?
How did it start to change?
I doubt if either of them really knows,

Or could pinpoint an hour, a day, a week
When things changed for them.
Perhaps part of the problem is that divorce is easy today.
Marriage is not thought of as permanent
The way my parents and grandparents thought about it,
Or the way my husband and I thought of it.
Breaking up and walking away is easier than staying and
   working through the problems.
However it happened
And whenever
And whoever's fault it was,
My daughter is hurting.
How can I help her, Lord?
I pray that You'll give her strength and courage
And peace.
I pray if there is a way to save this marriage, even now,
That You will show them both what it is.
I ask that You help my husband and me, too.
We still love our daughter
And our son-in-law, too.
We want them to know we love them.
Help us not to ask questions when we shouldn't,
Or to keep quiet when we should speak.
Don't let us be judgmental, Lord.
We have not walked in their moccasins
Or been on the path they took.
Help us to show our love for them
By not treating them as failures.
Give us the strength to hold up our heads with our friends,
   Lord,
Especially at church.
None of them have divorced children,
So they may not understand.
Don't let us take this too lightly, either, Lord,
Or too personally.
We did our best to raise our children to honor You
And their marriage vows.

This divorce is not our fault,
Even though Satan may try to make us think it is.
We can pray for wisdom and understanding,
But blaming ourselves is counterproductive.
We cannot help our daughter if we feel guilty ourselves.
It's a sad time for us, though,
Because our daughter is hurting
And we can't help her.
Eventually she will adjust, Lord,
And so will we.
But only with Your help.

She's My Little Sister,
And She's Dying, Lord

The call came tonight, Lord.
My sister is dying.
The doctor said this kind of cancer comes quickly
With almost no symptoms.
She is two years younger than I am, Lord.
At our ages two years isn't much,
But when we were small the difference seemed like a million to
   both of us.
I was the one who got to do everything first—
Going to school,
Having a birthday party,
Wearing a bra.
I always took care of her, Lord,
Protected her from the bigger kids,
And led her past the neighborhood dogs.
Now I can't break the path for her to follow, Lord.
She is going to do something first—
The biggest thing of all.
She is going to die before I do.
She will be the first of us to see You, Lord.
I can't help her.
I have to leave her care in the hands of strangers
And in Your hands, Lord.
I know she is safe there,
But I am going to miss her.
I remember the fun we had together when we were children.
We played with our dolls together,
Shared a bicycle,
And traded books and records.

We went on family picnics
And stuck together when our cousins started to tease one of us.
Oh, we had our differences, too.
Mother used to wonder aloud if we would ever grow up!
Even now we are not really alike.
She always liked artistic things, such as music, sculpture,
    and poetry.
I liked the out-of-doors activities, such as hiking, camping,
    and bird-watching.
Our children grew up together,
And we traded baby-sitting to help each other.
Part of my life will be gone when she goes, Lord.
You expect to lose your mother and father some day;
You expect them to die before you do.
You never think about losing people younger than you are.
Somehow, you expect them to be around forever.
Now I know she will not be here forever,
And there is nothing I can do to stop her going
Or to help her.
I can pray for her.
I ask You to be merciful and gentle with her.
Please don't let her suffer
Or know that she is causing her loved ones anguish as they
    watch her leave them.
I know she is not afraid to die, Lord.
She has been Yours since we were small.
You told us that whoever believes in You,
Even though she dies,
Will never really die,
But live forever.
Pain is something else.
Guide the doctors and nurses who care for her, Lord,
So that she will not suffer unnecessary pain.
Please keep her mind clear
So that she can say her good-byes to her family
And make her plans with them
And so she can pray.

She will need prayer now more than ever, Lord,
To give her the assurance and serenity she will need.
Bless her pastor, Lord.
It's not easy to comfort the dying;
There is the stark awareness of one's own mortality.
Be with her husband and children, Lord.
Make them strong in their faith
And brave in her sight.
Help me to be brave, too, Lord—
To comfort her and her family,
To tell her how much she means to me,
And how much I will miss her.
I know You told us You were going to prepare a place for us
And then come for us.
Come quickly, Lord,
And take my little sister home to be with You forever.

It's the Big "Five-O," Lord

Today I'm fifty, Lord,
    And it's a strange feeling to be a half century old.
I feel so young inside this body You gave me.
I know there are things I can't do anymore,
Such as climbing trees,
And doing a figure eight on skates.
But I really don't want to do those things anyway.
Today I'm looking back on my five decades, Lord.
I'm not rich or famous.
I haven't done anything outstanding for You or my neighbor,
    Lord.
I have tried to serve You and others in small ways,
When and where You showed me how to help.
I have learned so much, Lord, in these years,
About You, about others, and about myself.
I am past the "rushing" years of youth;
I know who I am now, Lord—
A child of God.
And I know what I can do well
And what I should leave to others.
I have much to thank You for, Lord.
I thank You most of all for your free gift of salvation
And the certainty that it is mine.
Thank You for my parents,
Who taught me about You,
And who sacrificed to give me advantages they never had.
Thank You for my brothers and sisters, Lord.
We had a lot of arguments and battles when we were young,
And we live far apart now.

Yet we know we are still a family,
And our love is strong enough to bridge miles and years.
Thank You for my husband, Lord,

And for our more than twenty-five years together.
I thank You for the worldly success You have allowed us,
The comforts we take for granted in our land and our home—
Things that would be luxuries to most of the world's people.
Thank You for the good times we've had
And for the harder times, too—
The times of sudden, serious illness
When we had to leave each other in the hands of strangers
In strange cities.
The times of standing together,
Watching over sick children with that helpless feeling parents
    have;
And the times of sorrow at the loss of two of our parents.
There was the bad time when a job was terminated
And we did not know there was a better one in the future.
Those bad days helped us grow, Lord—
Closer to each other
And closer to You.
Thank You for the children of our marriage, Lord,
And the happiness they have added to our lives.
We relive the days of their youth in memory now and then.
We remember driving to football games and hoping our son
    would play;
  And sometimes he did.
He's a man now, tall and true to You.
He's married to a girl we love
And the father of our first grandchild.
Thank You for our daughter, Lord.
We remember her first steps,
Her first day at school,
And her first date.
Now she's happily married to a fine man,
A success in her chosen career,
And the mother of our second grandchild.
Thank You for my friends, Lord.
There are friends whom I see every day,
Who come quickly in a crisis and who share my triumphs, too.

Thank You, also, for friends far away,
Who send their news in letters or tapes.
Bless them all, Lord.
Thank You for the world You have given me to live in,
And for the enjoyment I've had in learning about it.
I have seen the mountains, oceans, and sandy deserts.
Alone at night I have gazed at the skies so filled with stars
That they seemed to lie on top of one another.
I have spent time alone with You in Your Word
Or in Your house of worship.
Yes, I'm fifty today, Lord—the "Big Five-O," they call it,
And perhaps my life is two-thirds over.
Some of my friends tell me that this is the beginning of the end.
They say that from now on it will be aches and pains,
Problems too big to solve,
And loneliness.
They say I will slow down and nothing will be like it was.
They're pessimists, Lord,
And see only the worst that might happen.
There have been problems and limitations at every age, Lord,
And You've helped me through each one.
Why would You stop now,
Just because I'm fifty today?
I know there are many beautiful times in store, Lord—
Times of celebration with family and friends,
Times of anticipation and excitement,
Times of being able to help others because of my experiences in
    living with You,
Times of joy.
So I thank You in advance, Lord,
For the years to come—for both the joys and the sadnesses,
And for the faith to know You will always be with me,
Both in this world and the next.
Yes, I'm fifty today, Lord,
And thankfully eager to live the rest of my life as You want me
    to live.
It's a very happy birthday, Lord.

I Have Time for My Garden Now, Lord

I worked in my garden this morning, Lord,
All morning, without any interruptions,
Without feeling that I must hurry to do something else.
I could work at my own pace and do only what I wanted to do.
It was a wonderfully free feeling, Lord.
You know how many years I've planned this big garden in my
     mind.
I always knew exactly what flowers I wanted to plant,
And where I would plant each one so that I would have blooms
     from spring through fall.
You know how many seed catalogs I got in the mail each year,
And how I pored over them, studying and learning and dream-
     ing.
The problem back then was that we were raising children—
Not flowers.
Children were more important to us
Than the red and yellow and blue bouquets we have now.
Children need space—
Space to play kickball and baseball and football,
Space to run and jump and roll in the grass.
Children need the beauty of flowers, too, Lord,
And I always had a small garden near the house.
But never as big or with as many flowers as I really wanted.
Children take time and care, too, Lord,
And I spent my time and care on them when they needed me.
I had my own work outside the house then, too.
I did not have enough time to take care of a big garden.
Now, though, I have no children to take care of.
Now I do not have a job outside the house.

Now I have the time to grow my dream garden.
Now I can plant in the ground all the flowers
I have planted in my mind so often.
Now I can watch them bloom all season long.
I can take their sweet-smelling blossoms to friends
And use them to decorate the church some Sunday.
It was early when I got up this morning, Lord.
The sun was up, but without its heat yet.
Somewhere, a mourning dove was cooing softly.
The brown soil was soft, and moist, and cool after the night,
Almost as though it were alive, too.
Most women who garden wear gloves to protect their hands,
But I like the feeling of soil between my fingers.
I like to kneel and feel the dirt,
And marvel at how you planned that a tiny seed, dropped into
    it,
Comes up a strong plant, with beautiful flowers
And more than enough seeds to insure a new generation of
    flowers.
As I knelt with the soil in my hands, I felt close to You.
Someone once said we are closer to You in a garden than any-

    where else;
This morning I believed it.
I prayed as I dug, and weeded, and pruned.
I prayed for all those I love, Lord,
And for all Your people around the world.
I wished they could all be with me here in my garden.
It would bring peace to their hearts
And joy to their eyes.
A slight breeze moved, Lord,
Bringing me the mixed fragrances of the flowers.
It made me think of perfume—
The perfume the woman brought and poured on your feet,
    Jesus.
The woman Luke tells about in his Gospel.
I have read the story often, Lord,
And wondered about the woman.
I have thought about the banquet guests, too,
But I had never thought about the perfume before.
This morning I sat back on my heels and considered it.
Was that perfume made from flower petals?
Were the petals from flowers she had grown,
Or picked herself along the roadside
Or in the woods?
I dreamed of a perfume I might make from my flowers, Lord,
And how wonderful it would be to serve You personally
    with it.
But you know all about this dream, don't You?
My husband came out
And helped me with the last of the gardening.
We worked side by side,
Not saying much.
That's another nice thing about a long marriage, Lord;
We don't have to talk to communicate.
When we were finished and began picking up our tools,
He smiled at me.
"You're beautiful," he said,
And he kissed me—right there in my garden.

When you finish reading sign your name
inside front cover—then pass to another